25 Songs Arranged for Revival Choir
by Mosie Lister

Contents

A Name I Highly Treasure	115
A New Name in Glory	2
All Because of God's Amazing Grace	9
All the Way	33
Come and Dine	39
Dwelling in Beulah Land	65
Faith Medley	106
Faith Is the Victory	
I Know Whom I Have Believed	
We've Come This Far by Faith	
Free at Last	50
From the First Hallelujah to the Last Amen	13
I'd Rather Have Jesus	57
In My Risen Lord	101
It Is No Secret	19
It's Real	72
Light Up the Sky	24
My, Didn't It Rain	92
Pass Me Not—Medley	96
A Closer Walk with God	
Pass Me Not	
Redemption—Medley	81
Since I Have Been Redeemed	
Blessed Assurance	
To God Be the Glory	
Sing Praise to the King	120
Such Love	87
Unfailing Love	45
We Shall Overcome	62

Copyright © 1987 by Lillenas Publishing Co.
All rights reserved. Litho in U.S.A.

Lillenas Publishing Co.
KANSAS CITY, MO. 64141

A New Name in Glory

From the First Hallelujah to the Last Amen

Light Up the Sky

M. L.

MOSIE LISTER

©1974 and 1987 by Lillenas Publishing Co. All rights reserved.

Free at Last

R. R. and D. McG.
REBA RAMBO and DONY McGUIRE
Arr. by Mosie Lister

Joyfully ♩ = 76

© Copyright 1984 by New Kingdom Music/ASCAP. All rights reserved. International copyright secured.
Used by permission of The Zondervan Music Group, Nashville.

I'd Rather Have Jesus

RHEA F. MILLER

GEORGE BEVERLY SHEA
Arr. by Mosie Lister

Words © Copyright 1922, Renewed 1950, Music © 1938, Renewed 1966 by Chancel Music, Inc.
Assigned to The Rodeheaver Co. This arr. © 1987 by The Rodeheaver Co. (a div. of Word, Inc.).
All rights reserved. International copyright secured. Used by permission.

Dwelling in Beulah Land

Redemption Medley

Arr. by Mosie Lister

"Since I Have Been Redeemed" (Edwin O. Excell)

Arr. © 1987 by Lillenas Publishing Co. All rights reserved.

Copyright 1929. Renewed 1957 and arr. © 1974 and 1987 by Lillenas Publishing Co. All rights reserved.

My, Didn't It Rain

C. C. M.

C. C. MOURER
Arr. by Otis Skillings
Adapted by Mosie Lister

*These underlined words may be syncopated as in natural conversation.

Arr. © 1973 and 1987 by Lillenas Publishing Co. All rights reserved.

Pass Me Not—Medley

Arr. by Mosie Lister

*© 1987 by Lillenas Publishing Co. All rights reserved.

Arr. © 1987 by Lillenas Publishing Co. All rights reserved.

In My Risen Lord

M. L.
MOSIE LISTER

Faith Medley

Arr. by Mosie Lister

A Name I Highly Treasure

O. C. E.

OSCAR C. ELIASON
Arr. by Mosie Lister

Copyright 1946. Renewed 1973 by Lillenas Publishing Co. All rights reserved.

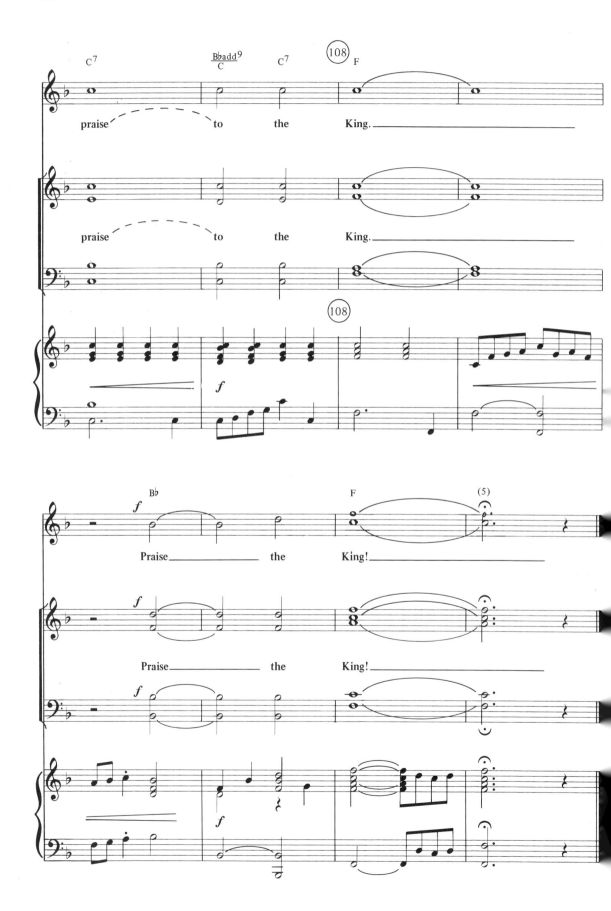